At the Gates of Dawn and Dusk

A Devotional for Aurora, Eos, and the Hesperides

Edited by Rebecca Buchanan

Copyright © 2018 by Neos Alexandria/Bibliotheca Alexandrina Incorporated

All rights reserved. No part of this book may be reproduced by any means or in any form whatsoever without written permission from the author(s), except for brief quotations embodied in literary articles or reviews. Copyright reverts to original authors after publication.

Front cover image: "At the Gates of Dawn" by James Herbert Draper; and interior images: "Memnon, Son of Eos and Tithonus" by Bernard Picart, "Cephalus Carried Off by Aurora" by Pierre Claude Francois Delorme; courtesy of wikimedia commons.

Verse for a Winter Solstice

by James B. Nicola

Though Eye can't see the sun at night
Heart recalls its velvet light
as Loss might, Love's, till Sleep, it seems,
consigns such warming orbs to dreams

where Mind persuades me that the burn
of caring may one day return —
"day" being symbolic of
such things as purpose, hope and love.

But years and decades are the en-
emy of hope to mortal men:
Winter's nights do not allow
in sunlight, or its memory, now.

Thank God the Mind knows one true thing:
That winter's depths shall yield to spring
as night to dawn, bedecked with dew-
drops, glimmering of hopes anew:

For in a moisture-clearing blink
I notice I've begun to think

Of you.

Eos Begins to Stir by Laurie Goodhart

Table of Contents

Verse for a Winter Solstice
 by James B. Nicola … 3
Eos Begins to Stir
 by Laurie Goodhart … 5
Introduction
 by Rebecca Buchanan … 10

Aurora and Eos
Cephalus Carried Off by Aurora
 by Pierre Claude Francois Delorme … 15
Aurora Speaks
 by Rebecca Buchanan … 16
Before the Gates
 by Chris Hubbard … 17
Daily Rites in Honor of the Lady and Her Sons
 by Rebecca Buchanan … 18
Dawn Devotions
 by John Opsopaus, Ph.D. … 22
Eos
 by Amanda Artemisia Forrester … 32
Ever-Shining
 by Zachariah Shipman … 33
Fingerpainting
 by Jennifer Lawrence … 34
Glorious Is the Dawn
 by Amanda Artemisia Forrester … 35

Hymn to Aurora
> by Iris ... 36

In Search of the Morning Star
> by Claire Manning ... 38

Eos on the Morning of the Eclipse
> *by Nina Kossman ... 47*

it is his cloak that catches her gleaming eye
> by Rebecca Buchanan ... 48

Lucifer Speaks
> by Rebecca Buchanan ... 49

Morning Prayer to Eos
> by Ariadni Rainbird ... 50

Mother of Crickets
> by Amanda Artemisia Forrester ... 51

Ode to Dawn
> by Zachariah Shipman ... 52

Praise to the Radiant Dawn
> by Gregory Stires ... 53

Prayer to Eos
> by Zachariah Shipman ... 54

Prayer to Eosphoros/Lucifer
> by Claire Manning ... 55

Three Hourglasses
> by Rebecca Buchanan ... 56

Titan
> by Gareth Writer-Davies ... 58

Vesper Speaks
> by Rebecca Buchanan ... 60

The Hesperides

The Hesperides
    by Nina Kossman ... 61
The Apple
    by Rebecca Buchanan ... 62
Bloody Sunset
    by Gerri Leen ... 78
Drakon Hesperios
    by Rebecca Buchanan ... 80
Fading Light
    by Zachariah Shipman ... 81
Hymn to the Hesperides I
    by Rebecca Buchanan ... 82
The Importance of the Evening Light in Hellenic Culture
    by Anne Hatzakis ... 83
Six A.M.
    by James B. Nicola ... 88

Memnon, Son of Eos and Tithonus
    by Bernard Picart ... 89

Appendix A: Public Domain Hymns to Aurora, Eos, and the Hesperides ... 90
Appendix B: Recommended Reading ... 102
Appendix C: Our Contributors ... 103
Appendix D: About Bibliotheca Alexandrina — Current Titles — Forthcoming Titles ... 110

Introduction

by Rebecca Buchanan

The Early-Born. She Who is the Morning-Twilight. Rosy-Fingered and Golden-Armed. The Saffron-Robed Goddess. Sister of Sun and Moon. Mother of the Winds and the Stars. Mother of the Morning Star and the Evening Star.

To the Romans, She is Aurora. To the Greeks, She is Eos. Put simply, She is the Goddess of the Dawn. But, as is always the case when dealing with Divinities, They are so much more than that.

A primordial Deity (not of the first generation but certainly older than the Olympians), She has links to the most basic elements of creation itself: light, time, movement, birth, and death.

Rising as She does every morning and settling beyond the horizon every dusk — without fail — Her devotees have also come to associate Her with hope, optimism, and perseverance. In later years, both the Dawn Goddess and Her sons (Heosphoros/Phosphorus and Hesperus in the Greek, Lucifer and Vesper in the Roman) came to be associated with freedom and enlightenment, especially in occult societies and writings.

Vivacious and lusty, She is a Goddess of renewal, dispenser of the dew which waters the fields every morning and the lover of many notable Gods, demigods, and mortals.

Few of Their affairs end well, though. In one tale, Eos carries off Cephalus and keeps him by Her side for eight years; when he is finally returned home, he accidentally kills his mortal wife, Procris. In another, Her lover Orion is killed by Artemis (why is up to debate). Mortal Tithonus is granted eternal life, but not eternal youth, and so he continues to age and shrivels up into a cricket. And, of Her many mortal children born to Her mortal lovers, it is said that She loved Memnon the most — and the dew is her tears, shed forever after his death on the plains of Troy. As such, there is more than a touch of tragedy and grief to this most evanescent of Goddesses.

As both distinct Goddesses and as poetic metaphor, Aurora and Eos appear frequently in Western literature. They have graced the works of Aeschylus, Björk, Charlotte Bronte, Corinna, Homer, Nonnus, Ovid, Sappho, Seneca, Shakespeare, Tennyson, Theocritus, Virgil, and Phillis Wheatley, to name just a very, very few. (It could be reasonably argued that Their appearances in art are even more frequent.) There has, however, been very little written about Them by modern Pagans and polytheists.

Heosphoros/Phosphorus and Hesperus — and Lucifer and Vesper — hold an unusual position in theology and poetry. The ancient Greeks and

Romans were quite well aware that the morning star and evening star were a single celestial object. As such, while it was associated with Aphrodite and Venus, respectively, it was *also* associated with the sons of the Dawn Goddess, and They were understood to be the same being called by different names at different times, according to His function (e.g., Cicero in *De rerum natura*). A philosopher seeking enlightenment might call on Heosphoros or Lucifer, while lovers begging night to come more quickly might call on Hesperus or Vesper.

Even less has been written about the Hesperides, who virtually disappear from Western literature after the arrival of monotheism. Daughters of primordial Night*, Goddesses of Dusk and Sunset and Evening, They live on an island beyond the western edge of the world, far out of the reach of ordinary mortals. Guardians of the treasures of the Gods, They keep watch over a Tree of Golden Apples, a wedding gift to Hera from Gaea Herself; as such, the Hesperides came to be known as Goddesses of brides and wedding nights, as well.

Though They make notable appearances in many of the classical world's most important myths (see the quest of Perseus, Herakles' eleventh labor, the voyage of the Argonauts, and the founding act of the Trojan War), They are never actors in their own tales; merely supporting players.

It is our hope that this anthology will right some of these wrongs, and begin to fill a notable gap in devotional literature. Through these poems, prayers, rites, and tales, we hope to awaken a renewed appreciation for Aurora, Eos, and the Hesperides; to inspire others to write and paint and sing and dance in Their honor; to hear Their names spoken aloud once again in love and devotion.

Rebecca Buchanan
EiC Bibliotheca Alexandrina
Winter 2018

* Ancient authors do not agree as to the parentage of the Hesperides. They are sometimes the daughters of Nyx alone, sometimes Nyx and Erebus, sometimes Atlas and Hesperis. Hesperus is sometimes named as the father of Hesperis, thus linking them back to Eos.

Aurora and Eos

Cephalus Carried Off by Aurora
by Pierre Claude Francois Delorme (1851)

Aurora Speaks

by Rebecca Buchanan

I descend to ocean's stream
from my rosy hall, and rise,
born anew. My love and my
grief are eternal, ever
staining my light. Gathering
the mists of morning, the dew
marks my passage, and my pain.

Before the Gates

by Chris Hubbard

At the gate of dawn I wait,
Patiently and fervent
Devoted and unwavering
Cast up the light from beneath the horizon
May the sun shine for us all

Pillars of light appear before me
Announcing your name
As you arrive into this world

Arched gateways appear before me
Knowledge once forgotten manifests with clarity

Each day, from darkness into light
Death and rebirth
Daily
Each day, I will stand in the East
And await your arrival
Each day, I will welcome your arrival
Into my life — bringing the dawn
Bringing a new day, bringing the mysteries
Which you guard
Into my heart

Daily Rites in Honor of the Lady and Her Sons
by Rebecca Buchanan

The following is intended to be a short, two-part rite which may performed every morning and evening. If necessary it can be performed at different times, but is best done at sunrise (or immediately after waking up) and at sunset (or immediately before bed). Please note that, while the names used here are generic, the rite may be modified and the proper names of the Greek or Roman Deities may be substituted.

Ritual Items
— an image of the Lady; ideally a statue or bust, but a print image works as well
— an image of the Morning Star
— an image of the Evening Star
— a small piece of saffron or rose-colored cloth
— a small piece of white or blue cloth
— a small piece of violet or black cloth
— a bowl of water
— a candle and matches, if the candle is not electric
— a flat surface where these items may be placed, such as an altar or box shrine
— you may also wish to add other items which you associate with these Deities, such as rose petals, images of horses and stars, images of lamps or torches, and so on

The Morning Rite

Upon rising, bathe or wash your hands and face. Stand before your altar. The image of the Lady should be draped, but not covered, by the saffron or rose-colored cloth; alternatively, have the image set on top of the saffron cloth. Light the candle. Say:

Greetings to you, Lady of the Dawn, and your Sons, the Morning Star and the Evening Star.

Cover the Evening Star image with the violet or black cloth. Say:

I thank you, Evening Star, for your many blessings and for watching over me and mine this night.

Remove the white or blue cloth from the Morning Star image. Say:

Morning Star, I thank you for your many blessings, and ask that you guide me and mine through this day. [Thank the Morning Star for any particular blessings. Also add any particular prayers for the coming day here, e.g. passing a test, success in a job interview, et cetera.]

Dip your fingers in the bowl of water and sprinkle the image of the Lady. Say:

Lady, as you guide the sun across the heavens, so I ask that you guide me and mine. As you bless this world with beauty and water, which allow life to flourish, so I ask that you bless me and mine. I thank you, Lady, for [insert particular blessings or thanks here]. *Fair travels, Lady.*

Pause for a moment or two. Meditate if you wish, or write, or perform other Work. Reverently extinguish the candle when you are done.

The Evening Rite

Bathe or wash your hands and face. Stand before your altar. Light the candle. Say:

Greetings to you, Lady of the Dusk, and your Sons, the Morning Star and the Evening Star.

Cover the Morning Star image with the white or blue cloth. Say:

I thank you, Morning Star, for your many blessings and for watching over me and mine this day.

Remove the violet or black cloth from the Evening Star image. Say:

Evening Star, I thank you for your many blessings, and ask that you guide me and mine through this night. [Thank the Evening Star for any particular blessings. Also add any particular prayers for the coming night here.]

Dip your fingers in the bowl of water and sprinkle the image of the Lady. Say:

Lady, as you guide the sun through the underworld, so I ask that you guide me and mine. As you bless this world with beauty and water, which allow life to flourish, so I ask that you bless me and mine. I thank you, Lady, for [insert particular blessings or thanks here]. *Fair travels, Lady.*

Pause for a moment or two. Meditate if you wish, or write, or perform other Work. Reverently extinguish the candle when you are done.

Dawn Devotions

John Opsopaus, Ph.D.

I write of Êôs (Ἡώς or Ἕως), goddess of the dawn, known as Aurora to the Romans, who is called Mistress (Potnia), Golden-throned (Khrusothronos), Saffron Robed (Krokopeplos), Rosy-fingered (Rhododaktulos), and Early-born (Êrigeneia). I will describe Êôs, goddess of the dawn, and explain how she brings the sun to the new day. Herein also are prayers and hymns to the Dawn Maiden.[1]

Êôs is the daughter of Hyperiôn, "the one above," who travels high above the Earth, and of Theia "the divine," or, according to others, of Euryphassa, the "widely-shining one," or of Pallas (and so she is called Aurora Pallantias, Aurora of Pallas). In any case, her parents are a sun god and a moon goddess, and she is a Titan of the second generation.

Êôs is young, highly spirited, and lovely; it is her nature to awaken desire. Her eyelids are snowy, her cheeks rosy and her head crowned with beautiful, dewy tresses. She has rosy arms and fingers and large, white wings. She wears a radiant crown or a star on her head, and sometimes she is veiled. Her robes are saffron yellow or dazzling white and purple, and she wears yellow shoes. She rides a rose-colored, purple, or golden chariot drawn by white horses. Or she may float in air, holding in each hand a pitcher, from which she pours the dew. Or again she may come riding on Pegasos and carrying a torch, for she requested Pegasos from Zeus after he punished Bellerophôn.

Tender-hearted Êôs is always eager for young mortal lovers; this is a punishment inflicted on her by Aphroditê for having slept with Arês. Like Aphroditê, she brings love to mortals, but is not so easily placated as the goddess of love. So also Dawn brings a renewal of erotic passions and the morning erection.

Êôs lives by the streams of Ôkeanos at the eastern end of the Earth. According to some, this is on Ortugia (or Dêlos), the Isle of the Rising Sun, where Apollôn and Artemis were born. The cocks call her in the morning, and she awakes and leaps eagerly from the bed of Tithônos, the deathless Trojan prince who is her husband. She leaves her court, glowing with rosy light, and opens the purple Eastern Gates of pearl upon the pathway strewn with roses. Swiftly she rides forth in her chariot drawn by two horses, Lampos (Shiner) and Phaethôn (Blazer), while Nux and Hupnos (Lat., Nox and Somnus, Night and Sleep) fly in front of her. Êôs lifts the veil of night and chases away the hosts of stars. (So also the souls of the dead depart at daybreak.) The first light of Dawn is white, for that is the color of her wings. Next we see the golden radiance from her saffron robe and yellow shoes. Finally her rosy arms and fingers stretch across the heavens. The flowers and plants, drenched by the dew that she pours from her pitchers, lift their faces to her in gratitude for the new day.

A fresh wind is felt at Dawn's approach, for Astraios, who is the dawn wind, and Êôs unite at dawn, to produce a fertilizing spirit. And so, by starry Astraios, she is the mother of the strong-hearted winds: brightening Zephuros (west), Boreas (north) — headlong in his course — and Notos (south). The remaining wind is Argestês (Bringer of Brightness), which is either Apheliotês (east) or Euros (southeast). These are the winds of morning, which bring benefits to mortals (as opposed to the other, turbulent, chaotic winds), for the beneficial winds are born of Êôs, "the eternally new light of the dawning day," and Astraios, "the luminous radiance of the night sky." The Four Winds help to organize human labor and to orient the sea lanes; they also define the cycle of the seasons.

To Astraios, the ancient father of the stars, she also bore the star Heôsphoros (Dawn-bringer) and the other gleaming stars by which the heaven is crowned. That is, the god of the night sky united with Dawn to engender the Morning Star (Heôsphoros). Others say that this Daystar, who is called also Phôsphoros (Lat., Lucifer) or Phaethôn (Illuminator), is the son of Êôs and Kephalos. In any case, carrying a torch he flies by his own wings before her chariot.

The Hindus say that Dawn (whom they call Ushas) is a young wife, who wakes her children and gives them new strength for the day's work. But because "to be awakened" is "to be wise," they also say she is the goddess who brings wisdom.

As the new day, Êôs accompanies her brother Hêlios, the Sun, throughout the day, riding or walking ahead of his chariot. Therefore she is identified with daylight and is called Hêmera (Day), Titô (cf. Titan < Day), and Hêlia; she is Queen of Day. Hêlios is preceded on his course by Selênê and Êôs, his sisters; Êôs is the wilder and more turbulent of the two. At dusk she accompanies the Sun to the west, where she is called Hespera (Evening). Yet again, as goddesses, Êôs, Hêmera, and Nux (Dawn, Evening, Night) are the Maiden, Mother and Crone. Observe: Selênê, Êôs, and Hêlios rule night, dawn, and day; their colors are the black of night, the red of morning, and the white of day. Alchemically they are quicksilver, salt, and sulfur; the quicksilver (silver Moon) and the sulfur (golden Sun) are united in the salt. Red Aurora's complementary partner, for whom she strives, is the green youth. Her dew is the elixir.

Dawn Prayer
(Ἡ Ἠῴα Λιτή, Preces Aurorae)

This has been my dawn prayer for more than twenty years; I've found it a great way to start the day. It is appropriate to pour a libation (perhaps of coffee!) for Êôs.

Close your eyes and visualize her actions at dawn (as described above). Then reach out your hand in salutation to the dawn and say:

I greet thee, Êôs goddess of the dawn,
who brings the newborn day; the stars are gone,
and fled before thy face; both Sleep and Night
are routed by thy torch, and put to flight.
The flowers are awakened by thy dew,
and turn toward the light, for you renew
their life; so also may thy dew revive
my soul today with thanks to be alive.
You care for all that's fresh and young,
so care for me, to whom thy dew has clung.
For you remind us that the darkest night
must yield to day and flee before the light.
I pray thee, shining Dawn, to bring to me
abundant wisdom, love, and energy.
I ask thee, gracious goddess, for a wealth
of hope, of time to do, of strength and health.
Especially, this day I ask of thee:
(fill in request) So may it be!
I give my thanks for all this day may bring,

all things embraced by Dawn and Evening.
Blow a kiss toward the dawn.

Hymns to Dawn
("Υμνοι εἰς 'Ηῶ, Hymni ad Auroram)

      I include here a few short hymns to Êôs, drawn from various sources.

I
Aurora is the first of all to wake;
she tramples over transitory night
the mighty Goddess, bringer of the light,
beholding every thing from Heaven's height,
the ever youthful, all reviving Dawn,
to every invocation she comes first.
      — adapted from a Vedic hymn to Ushas (Murray, 1895, p. 376)

II
Auspicious Êôs yokes her chariot from
afar, above the rising Sun, and she
comes gloriously unto men on many wheels.
      — adapted from a Vedic hymn to Ushas (Murray, 1895, p. 376)

III
Aurora, daughter born of Heaven, dawn
upon us with thy riches, spreading light,
and dawn upon us with abundant food;

delightful goddess, dawn on us with wealth.
— adapted from a Vedic hymn to Ushas (Murray, 1895, p. 376)

IV
Hail, gentle Dawn! mild blushing goddess, hail!
Rejoiced I see thy purple mantle spread
O'er half the skies: gems pave thy radiant way,
And orient pearls from every shrub depend.
— Somerville, quoted in Guerber (1921, p. 90)

V
[Ecce iam,] ecce vigil rutilo perfecit ab ortu
purpureas Aurora fores et plena rosarum
atria: diffugiunt stellae, quarum agmina cogit
Lucifer et caeli statione novissimus exit.
— sightly adapted from Ovid's *Metamorphoses* II.114ff.

VI
The vigilant Aurora opened forth
her purple portals from the ruddy East,
disclosing halls replete with roses. All
the stars took flight whilst Lucifer, the last
to quit his vigil, gathered that great host
and disappeared from his celestial watch.
— Ovid, *Met.* II.114ff, tr. Brookes More

Quotations

"Êôs who shines upon all that are on Earth and upon the deathless gods who live in the wide heaven." (*Theog.* 372ff)

"Now Dawn rose from her couch from beside lordly Tithônos to bring light to immortals and to mortals." (*Iliad* XI.1)

"Êôs the early-born was rising from deep-flowing Ocean, bringing light to mortals." (*Homeric Hymn to Hermes*, l. 184)

"For Huperiôn wedded glorious Euryphaessa, his own sister, who bare him lovely children, rosy-armed Êôs and rich-tressed Selênê and tireless Hêlios who is like the deathless gods." (*Homeric Hymn XXXI, To Helios*)

I also recommend Owen Meredith's poem in Guerber (1921, p. 72) and Tennyson's "Tithonus" (Gayley, 1921, pp. 177–9).

Endnotes

1) This chapter is adapted from a web page that I first posted more than twenty years ago, http://omphalos.org/BA/JO-DAL.html.

Sources

The foregoing mythological material is synthesized from a variety of sources:

Apollodorus (1921). *The Library*. 2 vols, trans. J. G. Frazer. Loeb Classical Library. Cambridge: Harvard Univ. Pr., sec. 1.4.4.

Bonnefoy, Y. (1992). *Greek and Egyptian Mythologies*, Trans. Wendy Doniger. Chicago: Univ. Chicago Pr., p. 210.

Carpenter, T. H. (1991). *Art and Myth in Ancient Greece*. London: Thames & Hudson.

Gantz, T. (1993). *Early Greek Myth*. Baltimore: Johns Hopkins Univ. Pr., p. 315.

Gayley, C. M. (1921). *The Classic Myths in English Literature and Art*, rev. & enl. ed. Boston: Ginn, p. 95.

Graves, R. (1955). *The Greek Myths*. Baltimore: Penguin, sec. 40.

Guerber, H. A. (1921). *Myths of Greece and Rome*. New York: Amer. Book Co., pp. 72, 90.

Hesiod, *Theogony*, ll. 372ff. In *Hesiod, the Homeric Hymns, and Homerica*, trans. H. G. Evelyn-White. Loeb Classical Library. Cambridge: Harvard Univ. Pr., 1926.

Homeric Hymn V, To Aphrodite, ll. 218ff. In *Hesiod, the Homeric Hymns, and Homerica*, trans. H. G. Evelyn-White. Loeb Classical Library. Cambridge: Harvard Univ. Pr., 1926.

Hornblower, S., and Spawforth, A, eds. (1996). *Oxford Classical Dictionary*, 3rd ed. Oxford: Oxford Univ. Pr., s.v. Eos.

Kerényi, C. (1951). *The Gods of the Greeks*. London: Thames & Hudson, pp. 192–205.

Kerényi, C. (1979). *Goddesses of Sun & Moon*, Trans. M. Stein. Dallas: Spring.

Guirand, F. (Ed.) (1987). *New Larousse Encyclopedia of Mythology*, Trans. R. Adlington & D. Ames. New York: Crescent.

Lemprière, J., and Wright, F. A. (1949). *Lemprière's Classical Dictionary*, new ed., London: Routledge, s.v. Aurora.

Murray, A. S. (1895). *Manual of Mythology*, rev. ed. Philadephia: David McKay, pp. 202–5, 376.

Nilsson, M. P. (1961). *Greek Folk Religion*. Philadelphia: Univ. Pennsylvania Pr., p. 5.

Oswalt, S. G. (1969). *Concise Encyclopedia of Greek & Roman Mythology*. Chicago: Follett.

Ovid, *Metamorphoses*, II.114, V.440. In *Ovid Metamorphoses*, 2 vols., trans. F. J. Miller. Loeb Classical Library. Cambridge: Harvard Univ. Pr., 1956.

Seyffert, O., Nettleship, H., and Sandys, J. E. (1901). *A Dictionary of Classical Antiquities*. New York: Macmillan, s.v. Eos.

Yonge, C. D. (1870). *English-Greek Lexicon*, ed. H. Drisler. New York: Harper & Bros., s.v. Aurora.

Eos

by Amanda Artemisia Forrester

Eos
Rosy-Fingered
Dawn-bringer
Dew-scatterer
Who heralds Her Brother Helios's approach
A coy smile on Her lips
Her beauty
Begins each day anew.
Eos of the Dawn,
I hail You.

Ever-Shining

by Zachariah Shipman

I am Eos,
Goddess of the Dawn.
Each day I ride across the sky,
Followed by my brother the Sun and my sister the
      Moon.
I bring the rosy hour of morning,
The magnificent radiance of Heaven
Shining like a beacon through the dark.
Ever-shining, am I.
Feast upon the brilliance of my light,
As I circle the Earth in my chariot.
Across the heavens,
I fly.
Ever-shining, am I.

Fingerpainting
by Jennifer Lawrence

As Apollo's chariot races from the stables,
Eos cracks open her pots of paint,
dips her fingertips into the cups of rosy pink,
shimmering gold,
draws arcs of gentian violet along the horizon;
great ragged sweeps of tangerine and coral,
then — waiting for the world to turn —
slender digits, tipped with smears of mauve and
        cream,
washes over all the sky's canvas
with sweet pale blue,
sending the mortals about their business
as dawn brings light and sight to the new day.

Glorious Is the Dawn

by Amanda Artemisia Forrester

Rosy fingers reach across the sky
From beyond the Horizon
Golden-haired Dawn proceeds slowly across the
    world
Shaking dew from Her fingers,
Carried in her goblet
Borrowed from Zeus' rains in starry heaven
A sly smile on Her lips
A coquettish shake in Her hips
Eos heralds Her Brother Helios' rising
Gentle Dawn, loved by all mankind
Who banishes the darkness of night
Filled with the terror of wolves and the biting cold
Eos brings the warmth of sun and spring and
    showers
Hail to Dawn, Rosy-fingered, rosy-cheeked, rosy-
    lipped!
Glorious is She Who banishes shadows and goes
before the Chariot of the Sun!

Hymn to Aurora

by Iris

Oh, Muses, please loose my tongue
That I may sing of the Bringer of Dawn!
Noble and lovely Aurora!
See how She dances across the sky
Ahead of Her beloved brother, the great Helios!
See how She paints the sky with rosy fingers,
Laughing in delight at Her sport!
Their sister Luna chuckles softly, amused,
As She sets that they may view Grandmother Terra.
Muses, let my heart's joy welcome Her!
Pink and yellow against a star-sapphire vault,
Brighter and brighter as They approach.
The farmer pauses in the milking to admire Her art,
The drunken stumbling home shake their heads
But She only giggles at their folly and brightens
       further.
Hear my praises, O laughing dancer!
Hear my joy in You, O noble herald!
You who love mortals, who delight in their voices!
You whose robes astonish the stars
So that they hide and veil their faces
Unable to compete with the glorious colors
Unable to match Your timeless beauty!
Surely Jupiter Himself strokes His beard,
Lest He betray a smile at Your antics!
Surely Sol loves following Your steps

And the colors You have created for the enjoyment
    of all!
You who warn of ill weather to the sailor,
You to whom the birds sing in reverence,
Bless us, each bright morning, with Your creations!
Remind us that each night ends by Your light!
Mighty are You, Dawnbringer, Aurora!

In Search of the Morning Star
by Claire Manning

*"Now in their age-old prison Aeolus
Had locked the winds, and brilliant in the dawn
The Morning Star had mounted high, the star
That wakes the world to work."* (Ovid 171)

My journey with the Morning Star began during a guided meditation. I was seeking out a Rebel deity as a part of my studies with the Temple of Witchcraft and Lucifer responded. It took me a while to figure out who I was talking to and what it meant for me and my practice, and it is that exploration which eventually led me to write this article.

As my experiences are only with Eosphoros, I will only be focusing on the Morning Star within this article. I will also be using the terms Morning Star, Eosphoros, and Lucifer interchangeably as to me they are all expressions of the same concept and names for the same deity.

The term Morning Star is generally used to refer to the planet Venus as it appears before the Sun in the morning. The earliest personification of Venus is that of Eosphoros (Dawn-Bringer) and Hesperos (Evening) in Greek mythology and literature, although the two were later combined and regarded as a single deity. Eosphoros became Latinized as Lucifer which translates literally as "light-bringer" (Eratosthenes and Hyginus 131) while Hesperos became Latinized as Vesper.

While there aren't any myths specifically about Eosphoros, there are a surprising amount of references in both Greek and Roman classical art and literature. Greco-Roman art tends to depict Eosphoros with an aureole, showing his stellar qualities, and frequently shows him with Hesperos, Eos, and/or Apollo.

Eosphoros' qualities, including his appearance, are greatly shaped by this and his role as the planet Venus. He is described as having "surpassed many others in beauty. In that regard he even rivaled Aphrodite … that is why it is called the star of Aphrodite and can be seen at both sunrise and sunset" (Eratosthenes and Hyginus 131).

Eosphoros was considered to be either the son of Cephalos and Eos (Eratosthenes and Hyginus 131) or of Astraeus and Eos (Hesiod 14). Servius proposed that Eosphoros was the father of the Hesperides whilst other writers suggest that Eosphoros was the father of Hesperis who became the mother of the Hesperides by Atlas.

The richest source of references to Eosphoros is likely Ovid's *Metamorphoses*. These references vary greatly, but can mostly be divided into two categories. The first deal with Eosphoros as the Morning Star creating a regular astronomical event that adds structure to the narrative, while the second group of references deal with the story of Ceyx and Alcyone.

Ovid's *Metamorphoses* repeatedly states that Eosphoros is the father of Ceyx and Daedalion. Several books of Greek literature tell the tragic love story of Ceyx and Alcyone who were either turned into birds for their arrogance (Apollodorus 38) or were separated by a shipwreck that claimed Ceyx's life (Ovid 266).

The *Iliad* continues the tradition of mentioning the Morning Star as an astronomical event when Homer states: "At the time when the Morning Star comes bringing news of daylight to the earth, and after him Dawn in her yellow robe spreads over the sea." (Homer 371)

In Aesop's *Fables*, Fable 211 speaks of a boastful lamp which claims to shine "brighter than the Morning Star" (Aesop 106) only to be swiftly extinguished by the wind. When the lamp is relit by a man he is told the error of his ways and asked to keep silent. This again shows that the Morning Star was used as a comparative fact within literature.

Seneca references Lucifer in both *Oedipus* and *Hercules Furens*. In *Oedipus*, Lucifer is used as a comparative fact within a prayer to Bacchus and then later to describe the shortened lives of soldiers on the battlefield describing their lives as "they rose when Lucifer was risen, and died when the Hesperides were not yet up" (Seneca 60).

In *Hercules Furens*, Seneca speaks of Lucifer in the lens of an astronomical event discussing the end of night and beginning of the dawn, stating "Lucifer leads off his sparkling troops … and summons day." (Seneca 144)

In *The Nature of the Gods,* Cicero argued several times that the planets, described as "those which stray" (Cicero 65), should be regarded as gods and admitted to the Pantheon. Cicero based his argument on the fact their observable behaviour stating "I cannot envisage such regular behaviour in the stars … as existing without intelligence, reason, and planning; and … it is impossible for us not to number them among the gods." (Cicero 66) He also draws upon the earlier writings of Balbus and uses that to support his argument pointing out the pre-existing inclusion of Apollo (the Sun) and Diana (the Moon) would naturally lead to the inclusion of other celestial bodies (Cicero 126).

After the decline of the Greek and Roman empires, Eosphoros' recognition continued, although the Latinized Lucifer became the preferred term of reference.

Most people will be familiar with the Christian concept of Lucifer as the Devil. This association has grown from a single passage which states "How you have fallen from heaven, morning star, son of the dawn! You have been cast down to the earth, you who once laid low the nations!" (*New International Version*, Isaiah 14:12). This view is mostly held by adherents of the King James-only movement who reject the newer translations of the Bible and will often reword passages to support their belief that Lucifer is the Devil (Wikipedia, Lucifer).

What is less familiar to most is that there are many references throughout the Bible that predominantly reference the Morning Star as an astronomical event without associating it with the Devil. Perhaps the most notable reference is found in *Revelation* 22:16 "I, Jesus, have sent my angel to give you this testimony for the churches. I am the Root and the Offspring of David, and the bright Morning Star." Thus creating an association between Jesus and the Morning Star.

Moving forward through time, Lucifer became the focus of the Romanian poem *Luceafărul* written in 1883 by Mihai Eminescu. *Luceafărul* is a philosophical love poem wherein Lucifer, referred to interchangeably as the morning and evening star, falls in love with a mortal girl and attempts to relinquish his immortality to join her, only for her to find another lover, at which point Lucifer rejects her and returns to the heavens.

The next notable mention of Lucifer is in Charles Leland's 1899 book *The Gospel of Aradia*. This claimed the existence of a legend from Tuscany in which Aradia, Queen of the Witches, was born or sent to Earth by her divine parents, Diana and Lucifer. The legend is repeated in Janet and Stewart Farrar's book *The Witches' God,* which states "Diana, the first of all creation, divided herself in two; the darkness was herself, and the light was her brother Lucifer. She desired him, but he fled from her as she pursued him round the heavens. Finally, by shape-changing into a cat, she got into his bed. He woke to find his sister beside him. From their union was born Aradia, the witches' teacher-goddess." (Farrar 198)

Whether Aradia actually existed is debatable, but many modern Wiccan and Pagan scholars, including the Farrars and Raven Grimassi, support this tale.

In modern times the majority of references to Lucifer are found in pop culture, which tends to draw on the later biblical mythos of Lucifer as the Devil. The CW's *Supernatural* has featured Lucifer as a recurring character in multiple episodes since Season 4 and *DC/Vertigo Comic*'s *Lucifer* has been adapted into a television show that has just been renewed for its third season. The show and comics feature Lucifer Morningstar as the king of hell who has moved to Los Angeles and splits his time between bar ownership and helping a homicide detective with her cases.

As with popular culture, most modern adherents of Lucifer draw at least in part on the concept of Lucifer as the Devil. Not all practitioners regard the Devil in a Christian sense, with most seeing it as an archaic concept representing putting yourself first. Lucifer is discussed at length in Anton LaVey's *Satanic Bible*, although LaVey and followers of his Church of Satan actually identify as atheists and do not recognize any deities. Other organizations that identify as Satanic, like the Satanic Temple, also identify as atheists.

Others work with Lucifer as the Morning Star and draw upon the earlier Greek and Roman teachings, seeing him as a light-bringing celestial God who is intrinsically linked with the qualities of Venus. In this regard, we can see him as a beautiful rebel who can cast light onto our work as witches and pagans. It is into this group which I myself fall.

Whether you call him Lucifer, Eosphoros, or simply the Morning Star, he can bring a great deal of illumination and light to your life and many blessings to your practice.

"The morning star revealed the shining day,
Night fled, the east wind fell, the rain-clouds
rose" (Ovid 171)

Citations

Aesop's Fables. Translated by Laura Gibbs, Oxford University Press, 2002.
Apollodorus. *The Library of Greek Mythology.* Translated by Robin Hard, Oxford University Press, 1997.
Cicero. *The Nature of the Gods.* Translated by P.G. Walsh, Oxford University Press, 1998.
Eosphoros & Hesperos. *Theoi.* 26 June 2017. http://www.theoi.com/Titan/AsterEosphoros.html

Eratosthenes and Hyginus. *Constellation Myths* with *Aratus's Phaenomena*. Translated by Robin Hard, Oxford University Press, 2015.

FAQ. *The Satanic Temple*. 30 June 2017. https://thesatanictemple.com/pages/faq

Farrar, Janet & Stewart. *The Witches' God*. Phoenix Publishing, 1989.

Hesiod. *Theogony* and *Works and Days*. Translated by M.L. West, Oxford University Press, 1988.

Holy Bible. New International Version, Hodder & Stoughton, 2011.

Homer. *The Iliad*. Translated by Martin Hammond, Penguin Books, 1987.

LaVey, Anthon Szandor. *The Satanic Bible*. Avon Books, 1969.

Luceafărul (poem). *Wikipedia*. 26 June 2017. https://en.wikipedia.org/wiki/Luceaf%C4%83rul_(poem)

Lucifer. *Wikipedia*. 28 June 2017. https://en.wikipedia.org/wiki/Lucifer

Ovid. *Metamorphoses*. Translated by A.D. Melville, Oxford University Press, 1986.

Phosphorus (morning star). *Wikipedia*. 28 June 2017. https://en.wikipedia.org/wiki/Phosphorus_(morning_star)

Seneca. *Six Tragedies*. Translated by Emily Wilson, Oxford University Press, 2010.

Eos on the Morning of the Eclipse
by Nina Kossman

it is his cloak that catches her gleaming eye

by Rebecca Buchanan

red
amidst a field
of white blooms

hair dripping salty water
from her bath in ocean's stream
she descends
bare-breasted
skirt of mist and dew
draped 'round curving hips

amores flock
summoned by her divine sigh
pluck tender blossoms
braid them through golden curls
as she gathers him close
still sleeping
dreaming
of his bright-eyed wife

[after "Cephalus Carried Off by Aurora" by Pierre Claude Francois Delorme]

Lucifer Speaks

by Rebecca Buchanan

Harbinger of dawn, I wake
the world. Bright-eyed, I bear the
torch of enlightenment. I
marshal the stars, plotting the
course of sun and zodiac.
I am the philosopher,
seeking, ever questioning.

Morning Prayer to Eos

by Ariadni Rainbird

O beautiful Goddess whose gentle light
Chases away the vestiges of night
Your rosy fingers paint the sky
With glorious hues, spreading high
Refreshing, cleansing, golden light
Heralding the Sun, most bright
Shake the sleep from heavy eyes
And bless this day, O Goddess wise
That we may rise like the Blessed Sun
And shine forth 'til our work is done
May Dawn's gentle breeze ever blow
Blessings upon us that help us grow
Bless our work and all we do
We dedicate this day to You
Let us rise refreshed this morn
O lovely Goddess of the dawn

Mother of Crickets

by Amanda Artemisia Forrester

Great Titaness, Eos-Aurora
Sister of the Moon and Sun
Radiant Mother of the Winds and of Stars
Winged Lady, with golden tresses braided
Chaser of starry Orion, the mightiest hunter
Cursed by Aphrodite to always burn with lust
She steals away handsome young sons
Consort of fair Tithonos – Oh, the folly!
To ask Father Zeus to grant Your lover eternal life,
And neglect necessary youth!
And so as the ages wore on, the poor shepherd lad succumbed
This body ravaged by Geras
Shrinking and wrinkling and folding in on itself
Until he is nigh unrecognizable.
Still he sings his nightly songs,
chirp chirp chirp
And so the race of crickets is born.
So I name you, Shining Eos, another name,
Consort and Mother of Crickets,
In honor of poor ill-fated Tithonos.
May he always be remembered.

Ode to Dawn

by Zachariah Shipman

Without you,
There is no morning,
There is no joy,
Simply the empty void of night!
There is no warmth,
There is no shine,
Without the fruitful comings of thine sweet Helios!
Each morning you rise,
Each night you vanish,
Come quick again!

Praise to the Radiant Dawn

by Gregory Stires

Golden Eos, may you hear my voice filled with
      reverence for you.
It is you who announces the start of every new day.
Ascending from Oceanus with feathered wings of
      red hues,
The Horae and Hesperos are at your side as you
lead the way for Helios in his golden chariot.
Mother of the stars of whom no words can describe
      your radiance.
Mother of the winds, you leave all breathless at the
      sight of your perfection.
I praise you, Eos, you who nourishes the earth with
      morning dew,
You who holds dominion over new beginnings, for
you are the one who announces the start of the day.
Eos, you whose radiant light is deathless, for it
shines brighter as time passes on. Thank you,
radiant Eos, for the splendorous gifts you bestow
      upon us mortals.
May your radiant light shine ever brighter.

<u>Prayer to Eos</u>

by Zachariah Shipman

Eos,
Goddess of the Dawn,
Bringer of the Sun!
Shine your brilliant light,
You who ends the night!
Daughter of Hyperion and Theia,
Rosy-fingered mother of the winds,
Sister of Sun and Moon!
Bless us this morning with joy,
And fill our weary hearts with peace!

Prayer to Eosphoros/Lucifer
by Claire Manning

O great Morning Star,
Known as Eosphoros to the Greeks
and light-bearing Lucifer to the Romans.
I call to you in honour and reverence.

Beautiful Venusian Prince,
wandering star, bearer of light.
Lend me your gift of illumination
and radiate your light into my life.

Herald of dawn, marshal of the starry host.
Awaken me to your mysteries
and help me grow closer to you.
With blessings and grace, so mote it be.

Three Hourglasses
by Rebecca Buchanan

Aurora
Beloved of gods and men, I am
mother of beauty and grief.
I renew myself
in ocean's
stream,
gathering
morning's dew. Saffron-
robed, I throw wide the golden
gates of heaven and call forth the sun.

***

Lucifer
Father of enlightenment, spark of
illumination, I hide
my grief behind the
weeping clouds.
I
am the star
who wakes the dawn. Last
to leave the morning sky, I
guide the stars as they seek their day's rest.

***

Vesper

Father of silence, the angel of
contemplation, I am the
fairest star. The last
light of day,
I
herald the
night. Twilight-robed, I
escort the sun to the gates
of heaven and shepherd the stars home.

Titan

by Gareth Writer-Davies

to spread a crack and let in the dawn
is hard work

the type of shift
that cleaners and truckers, never quite get used to

breathing hard
across the cosmos, like Axanimines
(who conjectured a frisbee shaped sun)

Eos eases
back the gates of heaven's factory

blushed
sweaty like dew

her lover's bed
somewhere back yonder

as the sun
explodes like a bomb

winged
by arrows

Eos
flips down her shades

trims
her diadem

tomorrow
will be another early rise for Titan

Vesper Speaks

by Rebecca Buchanan

I am the shadow dancer,
violet-wingéd. I am
the forerunner of twilight,
leading night across the sky.
I close the gates of heaven
behind the sun and shepherd
the stars to their proper place.

The Hesperides

The Hesperides
by Nina Kossman

The Apple

by Rebecca Buchanan

The apple lay on the sidewalk, glinting, just on the edge of the circle of light cast by the streetlamp. A thin layer of snow surrounded it.

Gary stared down at the apple, shoving his hands deeper into the old army jacket. He looked up, head swiveling back and forth as people rushed around him, talking rapidly on phones, or with their faces buried in scarves and coat collars. How had no one else seen the apple?

Too busy.

Or maybe no else was hungry enough.

Thanking his lucky stars, Gary bent and picked up the apple.

It was round and firm between his fingers, not a dent or blemish on its smooth golden skin. It smelled sweet, though not overripe. Perfect.

He lifted it to his lips, inhaling the scent.

"Be very certain before you take a bite."

Gary stilled, the apple between his teeth. His eyes jumped around, trying to locate the voice. He finally found her just to his left, just outside the circle of light.

He blinked, arm slowly lowering to his side.

She was naked.

Well, not quite, but pretty close. A red and gold cloth — some kind of fancy silk? — draped her hips, held in place by a wide golden belt. Bright red flowers in a dozen different shades circled her ankles and were knitted through her deep golden hair. Her feet were bare. And a thin green snake looped around her neck, its head curling around her right breast.

Its tongue flicked out, skipping across her nipple.

She smiled at him, an expression that seemed equal parts resigned and exasperated.

"Uh," he said.

"They do this sometimes, the apples. Fall off the tree and into the world. Arethusa is convinced that it is the natural order of things, as fruit does fall from trees when it ripens. Erytheia believes that Gaia is responsible, or perhaps Hera, or even Athena or Aphrodite; she can't make up her mind." She tilted her head at him, one hand lifting. The snake arced forward, curling around an extended finger. "I think they are both right, one Goddess or another sending the apple where it is needed — after all, it did find *you*."

Gary swallowed hard, looking around. People continued to rush by as night thickened and the snow fell harder, completely ignoring him and the nearly nude woman with her pet snake.

His stomach rumbled.

"Take care. There are consequences to eating that particular apple. Here." She extended her hand, the snake sliding forward to wrap around her wrist and forearm. A crisp one hundred dollar bill rested in her hand. "This will buy you plenty of apples."

He swallowed hard again, licking his lips. He reached for the money. Hesitated, fingers curling. The snake flicked its tongue. He dropped his hand, lifted it again, dropped it.

"What, uh … what do you mean by *consequences*?"

She was silent for a long moment, hand still extended. The bill disappeared and her hand descended gracefully to rest on her hip. The snake undulated, weaving around the belt, sliding across her belly. "The apple found *you*," she repeated. "Take a bite, and you will know why, and you will never escape that knowledge. Take a bite, and the tree will know *you*, in turn, and more apples will fall and find you. You will never escape them or what the Goddesses require of you — whichever Goddess needs you at that moment." She quirked an eyebrow and drew a sheaf of golden hair across her shoulders with one hand. "Perhaps your lucky stars *are* lucky and it will be Hebe and all she will need you to do is deliver a message to a pouty teenage girl. But I very much doubt that."

She moved forward a step, then two, feet barely seeming to skim the snowy ground. Her hips swayed. Her eyes traveled up and down his body, taking in the beat up boots, the old jeans, the army jacket and backpack that still had Darby's name and rank. She lifted a hand, gently resting the tips of her fingers near the bullet scar on his left temple.

For the first time, he noticed that she smelled just like the apple.

Her hand curled around his cheek, thumb brushing the beard that he had let grow too long. "Given who you are, though, I suspect Athena or Hera. They favor heroes."

He snorted, the sound turning into an ugly laugh. He backed away a step, out of her reach. "Not a hero. Never been one."

Her hand lifted again, palm up. "Then give me the apple."

He swallowed hard, fingers convulsing around the fruit. "What if I do? Give it back."

She shrugged, an elegant roll of her shoulders. "Perhaps nothing. The task which needs to be done will remain undone because only you could complete it. Or, another apple will fall and another hero will be found and the world will go on and you will return to your hunger and your nightmares."

His whole body twitched. "Don't hold back do you?"

"I have eternity. The world does not. Choose."

The snake held still.

He lifted his hand, letting the apple roll into his palm. It seemed plain enough, ordinary enough.

Just an apple, though perfectly ripe and sweet-smelling. Just an apple.

Hero.

The recruiter had called him that, and his parents. His sister, too, and his CO and all those girls who had been taken and who would have been sold off if his unit hadn't stumbled into that cave. But all the girls hadn't made it out and neither had Darby and he could still hear the screams and taste the dirt and the blood in his mouth.

But they had still called him a hero. Pinned a medal on his chest. But the medal didn't keep the nightmares away, and his parents could only hug him so hard. So he took Darby's jacket and his bag and ran, and kept running, and the nightmares still followed.

He swallowed, trying to find his voice. "What's this thing, this job, that needs to be done? What is it?"

"I don't know."

He inhaled. His hand was shaking. "But it's important, yeah?"

"Yes." The snake slowly uncurled from around her waist and began making its way up her arm.

"Will the nightmares go away? If I do this — whatever this is — can you make them stop?"

A long pause. "It is not my task. You are not my chosen hero. I cannot speak for the one who sent you the apple."

This time he laughed outright, a harsh, almost bitter sound. "So, you're saying that I could end up with more nightmares. Or minus a hand. Or dead."

"Such is the nature and necessity of heroes. To do what must be done. Choose."

The little girl in the cave, clinging to him and crying as he shielded her from bullets and splinters of rock. Darby yelling at him to get out, get her out, he would cover them ….

He was no hero. Darby was the hero. Darby was dead.

For Darby.

He bit into the apple. The taste and texture and juice filled his mouth, spread across his tongue. Another bite, and another as he devoured the apple.

It tasted like sunset. Hot reds, spicy oranges, tart yellows, a touch of cool and sweet blue.

And he knew. He knew who had chosen him, and why, and what he had to do. He knew who he had to save. And he could. He would.

He crunched down on the core, swallowing the last of the apple, and looked up.

The woman was gone.

No. Not a woman. A Goddess. Aigle. *Radiance.* He knew her name now.

Shifting the backpack on his shoulders, he set off through the night and the snow, running.

***

Brandon Franks. Age seven years, four months, and thirteen days. School was out for a long weekend, so he hadn't eaten in three days. His mother had thrown him out of the house for trying to sneak a cookie from her secret stash. It was below freezing now, well after dark, and he sat huddled behind the trash cans, pressed up against the side of the house next to the dryer exhaust, dressed only in jeans and a thin shirt.

By the time Gary found him, chest heaving, Brandon's lips and fingers were blue and he was unconscious.

Brandon Franks, who would grow up to found a charity for abused children, who would save thousands of lives, who would write legislation, testify before judges and Senators and Representatives, who would adopt five children himself and give them a home where they were loved and nurtured —

— but only if he grew up.

Gary ripped off Darby's jacket, wrapping Brandon up tight. He pulled the small camping blanket out of the backpack and wrapped that around him, too (small, he was too small and thin). Pulling the boy into his arms, he ran down the alley, knees aching, dodging feral cats and trash cans.

The gas station. There was a gas station on the corner.

He shoved through the door, shouting for help. The twenty-something blonde girl behind the counter squeaked and scrambled for a phone while a black guy with grey curls dug the portable heater out of the back office and turned it on full blast.

The police came. An ambulance came. They dumped Darby's jacket and the blanket on the floor. Gary quietly picked them up, shot one last look at little Brandon as they loaded him onto the stretcher, and slipped out the door.

***

He was on the news the next day. He caught a few seconds of grainy footage while he stood in line at the mission. The sound was off, but the closed captioning had been turned on. Gary picked out a word here and there, dividing his attention between the news and the smiling volunteers doling out hard buns and bowls of chicken noodle soup. *Boy rescued ... child services ... unknown good samaritan ... anyone with information ....*

He ate quickly, his head down, tucked a few extra buns in his pockets, and left the mission.

***

Early spring. Rain mixed with snow that melted almost as soon as it hit the ground.

This time the apple was sitting on a bench inside a bus shelter. Four other people huddled there waiting for a ride downtown and none of them saw it.

He picked it up gently, lifting it to his nose to inhale the scent.

"Are you absolutely certain?"

She was outside the shelter. The rain didn't touch her. A nearly sheer red dress, buttoned at the shoulders and embroidered with gleaming gold thread, fell to her bare feet. Her golden hair was piled high and dotted with flowers, loose curls dancing around her cheeks. The snake circled the crown of her head, a hissing, shimmering wreath.

"I get a choice?"

"You always have a choice."

"What about — you know — *the tree knows me*, and all that?"

Aigle held out a hand to her side, palm up. The rain which had not touched her collected in her palm. The snake slithered down her arm, tongue darting out as it lapped delicately at the water. "The tree does know you. So does She who chose you. You are more likely to say yes, then no. But you can still say no."

He hesitated, licking his lips. "Brandon. He's … okay, right?"

Aigle tilted her head, seeming to consider for a moment. "He is scarred and has nightmares. The scars will never completely heal, but the nightmares will fade. He will be able to sleep. He will show the scars to his children, so that they know that he understands, and they will come to trust and love him."

Gary inhaled sharply, and bit into the apple.

***

Stefanie Nevis. Twenty-three years, six months, two days. Graduate student in art history. She will dedicate her life to recovering, restoring, and protecting the world's most endangered art, even going so far as to set up a clandestine network for the purpose of smuggling at-risk art out of war zones and away from hostile regimes. She will be imprisoned once, shot twice, threatened with rape and death on multiple occasions, and address the United Nations.

If her ex-boyfriend doesn't kill her and bury her in his basement.

Gary shoved him down the stairs of Stefanie's apartment three minutes before she returned from class.

***

There were three more apples over the course of the year. Each time, Aigle appeared, radiant and questioning. *Are you certain? Are you sure? Do you consent? You can always say no.*

He bit the apple. Always. Every time. And each time it tasted like sunset and the knowledge of who he is supposed to save and why filled his mind, makes his chest pound and his blood rush.

He got a knife in his left shoulder saving Dana Pepper during a convenience store robbery. He left before the EMTs and police arrived, and woke up hours later in an alley, the snake curled around his throat. There was a scar and his jacket was torn and bloody. The snake disappeared.

He broke his thumb and scraped both knees shoving a future high school principal out of the way of a drunk driver, and burned his hand rescuing a pharmaceutical technician from a fire (she would blow the whistle on diluted chemotherapy drugs).

There were four apples the year after that, then five, six. More apples every year. He moved from city to city, stayed a week or a year, going where he was sent, where he was needed.

The nightmares lessened. Most nights, curled up in a park or a shelter, he slept. Sometimes, he dreamt about Darby and the cave and the girls and he woke up sweating and shivering. Other nights, the dreams were better, happier: Darby trying to steal his bacon the first day of basic training, Darby laughing at some stupid cat video, Fourth of July with his parents and sister, his mom's dry turkey at Thanksgiving.

Ten apples, eleven, fifteen, eighteen. Three years, five, six, ten, twelve.

***

Hoshi Jones. Sixteen years, six months, six days. Math whiz and astronomy nut. Destined to solve Baryon Asymmetry and found a chair in astrophysics at Stanford. If he isn't killed in a drive-by shooting while picking up diapers for his baby sister.

Gary was late. Almost too late. Three bullets ripped into him, one tearing through his right side to punch through into Hoshi Jones' left arm as he tackled the kid to the ground. A second bullet tunneled through his left bicep, ripping meat and shattering bone, before exiting, only to bounce off a street lamp and flatten itself against the sidewalk. The third skimmed the side of his head, leaving a deep gouge right above the scar he earned all those years ago in that cave.

He passed out, blood filling his abdomen.

He woke up in the hospital three days later, minus part of his liver and a short section of his intestine. His mother was asleep in the chair beside his bed, and he knew that the coat hanging on the wall belonged to his father because the ratty plaid scarf dangling out of the pocket was the same scarf that his father had worn for as long as Gary could remember.

And Aigle was there, sitting on the side of his bed. She was in dark red jeans, a wide golden belt around her waist. She wore her deep golden hair in two thick braids that hung over her shoulders. She tickled the snake with the end of one braid while she watched him.

"Hoshi?" he panted. His chest doesn't want to fill with air. "Okay?"

"He will require physical therapy. After he returns to school, his mother will make him wait to leave until she gets off work and can walk him home. He will spend that hour trying to solve various unsolvable problems in physics. He will eventually solve at least one." She tilted her head, gaze sinking away for a moment. Then she focused on him again, smile radiant. "Perhaps even three, if he remembers to take his pencil sharpener. Won't that be extraordinary?"

His mother mumbled and shifted in her chair.

Gary stared at her for long moments, lost at the sight of her gray hair and the lines around her mouth and down her cheeks.

His father had begun to lose his hair when Gary left, when guilt and nightmares drove him away. He wondered if his father was bald now, if he was still trying to write that definitive history of deep sea fishing, if his sister ever settled on a degree or kept changing her mind, if she got married, if she had kids, if ….

He didn't realize that he was crying until Aigle's hand settled on his cheek, her thumb wiping away a tear.

"Ah, my warrior, you are so tired."

The pain and tightness in his chest eased. He was finally able to draw a full breath, filling his lungs. "Apple. Just … give me a few days, and then send me another."

Her hand fell away, her fingers curling together in her lap. The snake hissed, circling her throat. "*I* do not send the apples. And wouldn't you rather return home?"

He shook his head, the movement making him dizzy. He quickly stopped. "No."

One elegant eyebrow jumped up. "No?"

"No. I — can't. I need — I need to save them."

"How many? How many do you need to save?"

"All. I need —" He was gasping again. "Need to save all of them."

"Why? Because you couldn't save one? Because your friend died saving you?"

"Yes—!"

"Well, that is just idiotic."

Gary's mouth fell open. He stared at her.

"Well it is," Aigle insisted. "It is really quite stupid, and silly, and sad. You mortals. I mean, *really*." The snake slid down her arm, undulating across his thigh and abdomen. "Darby died. It happened. It is done. His death was not and never will be anyone else's death. Nor will his life, the one that he lived or the one that would have been, whichever of an infinite number of paths he chose.

It was unique. He was unique. Saving another will not undo his death. Saving another means precisely that: saving *another*. A different mortal. A different life. A different unique being whose steps will fall upon one of an infinite number of potential paths. Take joy and solace in *that*, my idiot hero. In the lives that you *have* saved — singular, beautiful, and irreplaceable."

He was weeping, great, heaving sobs that shook his whole body. His face was wet, tears streaming down his cheeks to splatter and roll down his chest, turning his hospital gown a darker shade of blue. He curled his shoulders, tucking his chin as Aigle's arms wrapped around him. Her fingers threaded through his hair, gentle and comforting.

"It is time to rest. The apples will continue to fall and heroes will continue to rise, as it has always been. But it is time for you to go home." He felt her smile against the top of his head. "Say yes."

He gave a broken nod, hiccuping and panting.

"Yes," he said.

***

Brandon Franks dashes up the steps of his dormitory. Twenty minutes until his psychology class, and then his social work class immediately after that. He has just enough time to run up to his room, swap out his textbooks, and grab a granola bar and milk for the road.

Waving to a few classmates, he digs his key out of his pocket and shoves open the door of his room. He flips on the light switch, dumps his backpack onto his desk, and makes a beeline for the mini-fridge at the foot of his bed. Single serving of milk, check. Two granola bars, check.

Straightening, he turns back to his bag.

There is an apple sitting on the desk, right next to his backpack. It catches the light slipping in through the window blinds, gleaming.

Brandon frowns. Picking it up, he inhales deeply.

"Be careful." Her voice, like an evening breeze, fills the room. "There are consequences to eating that particular apple."

Bloody Sunset

by Gerri Leen

Hera's apples of gold, shining
Strong and bright and full
Of a bride's regard for
Her one true love
Unfortunately, she wasn't
His one true love

"Heracles seeks the apples," she says
Admiring the gifts bestowed on Zeus
"We will guard them well"
We rush to assure, one then the others
Her smile is frightening
"Do not trouble yourselves"

She is our queen, so we wait
And we hear her laughing
From far Olympus as the blood
Of the defeated and the slain
Weighs down the essence of the Apples
Till they are drenched in it

The sky that night is red, not gold
And as Atlas takes the apples from us
Heracles' face imprinted on the heavens
In traces of gold and pink and orange
We know they cannot stay with mortals

They burn too brightly, their juice now caustic

Hera waits as Athena brings them back
She stops the Wise One from chiding us
"They only did as I asked
Once these mirrored my love for Zeus"
They drip blood even as their skin gleams whole
"Now they mirror my husband's for me"

Athena cannot argue so she flees
Atlas groans, held fast under the world again
Tricked, as we all were, but not by Heracles
By this queen who normally hates Heracles so
"We are all pawns of someone"
She holds the apples to her breast, her eyes dry

Drakon Hesperios
by Rebecca Buchanan

we dance 'round the tree
and the serpent sings
from a hundred throats

the serpent sings his
songs of dusk and death
tongues caressing fruit

dusk and death he sings
shedding his scales of
red gold gleaming blue

he sheds his bright scales
reborn each dawn as
we dance 'round the tree

Fading Light

by Zachariah Shipman

We are the Hesperides,
Goddesses of the evening sun,
Matrons of the fading light.

Sunset marks the end of day, and the arrival of
    Selene.
Her bright luminescence follows the golden glow of
    Our aura,
Just as Helios follows His sister over the horizon.

We guard the Gods' treasures within our garden.
Here, we dance and frolic and play.
We drink with the joy of Dionysus.

We delight in our ecstasy, pleasuring ourselves
    freely,
But we are lonely,
Desiring the company of men.

We circle mighty Atlas,
We matrons of the fading light.

Hymn to the Hesperides I

by Rebecca Buchanan

they are the evening dancers, the
dragon maids, daughters of ancient night,
who guard the golden apples, gift of
earth to the queen of olympus, who
aided heracles in his epic
quest, mortal destined for godhood, who
make their home in the garden of the
west, the song of dusk on their tart lips

The Importance of the Evening Light in Hellenic Culture

by Anne Hatzakis

From the classical period to the modern era, the Hellenic culture has preserved the importance of the evening, and especially, the evening light in cultural and religious thought. Before I go into the pre-Christian aspect of this cultural continuation, I would like to share a hymn from my childhood as an Orthodox Christian. It is the Φῶς Ἱλαρόν, *Fós Ilarón* (*O Gladsome Light*) and is the oldest extant Christian hymn outside of the Bible that is still in use today.

Φῶς ἱλαρὸν ἁγίας δόξης ἀθανάτου Πατρός,
οὐρανίου, ἁγίου, μάκαρος, Ἰησοῦ Χριστέ,
ἐλθόντες ἐπὶ τὴν ἡλίου δύσιν, ἰδόντες φῶς ἑσπερινόν,
ὑμνοῦμεν Πατέρα, Υἱόν, καὶ ἅγιον Πνεῦμα, Θεόν.
Ἄξιόν σε ἐν πᾶσι καιροῖς ὑμνεῖσθαι φωναῖς αἰσίαις,
Υἱὲ Θεοῦ, ζωὴν ὁ διδούς· διὸ ὁ κόσμος σὲ δοξάζει.

Transliteration (into reconstructed Classical Greek pronunciation as opposed to that of the time period in which it was written)

Phôs hilaròn hagías dóxēs, athanátou Patrós,
ouraníou, hagíou, mákaros, Iēsoû Christé,

elthóntes epì tèn hēlíou dýsin, idóntes phôs hesperinón,
hymnoûmen Patéra, Hyión, kaì Hágion Pneûma, Theón.
Áxión se en pâsi kairoîs hymneîsthai phōnaîs aisíais,
Hyiè Theoû, zoèn ho didoús, diò ho kósmos sè doxázei.

Verbatim Translation
O Light gladsome of the holy glory of the Immortal Father,
the Heavenly, the Holy, the Blessed, O Jesus Christ,
having come upon the setting of the sun, having seen the light of the evening,
we praise the Father, the Son, and the Holy Spirit: God.
Worthy it is at all times to praise Thee in joyful voices,
O Son of God, Giver of Life, for which the world glorifies Thee.[1]

As you can see, the evening light was attributed to the new God being worshipped by the Byzantine Christians, but the first words were still talking about the holy nature of the light and praising not only the ending of the day, but the beginning of the new one as both the Jews and Greeks of the period actually counted the day as beginning at sunset, unlike the Romans who began their day at sunrise, or indeed modern people who count the day as beginning at midnight.

This speaks to the deep importance that the evening light had for the Hellenes of the pre-Christian period because a hymn like this would not have been written if that importance had not existed. And it is interesting that it is dedicated to a Trinity of beings instead of being like some of the other early Christian hymns that emphasize Jesus or the Holy Spirit.

This, to me, mirrors the classical Hesperides who guarded the Golden Apples of Hera. In myth, they were either the daughters of Nyx (Night) or Atlas by Hesperis. I tend to favor the first because of two reasons. The first is that there are more sources in the mythography for this ancestry; the second because there is a natural and visible connection between evening and night.

The Hesperides in ancient art are depicted as bringing ambrosia to the Theoi at feasts such as the marriage of Thetis to Peleus. The apples they guarded were the ones that Gaia gave to Hera on her marriage to Zeus. Apples were considered by the Classical Greeks to be a sacred fruit for marriages, and as such the guardians of the tree of Hera's Golden Apples would be of great importance.

This importance is reflected in their names. The names that they were called by as the daughters of Nyx were: Αιγλη/Aegle (Sunlight, Radiance),

Ερυθεια/Erythea (Red), and Ἑσπερεqουσα/Hesperethusa (Evening-Swift) which are reflective of the way that the evening light appears.[2] Some alternate names that they were called by were: Λιπαρα/Lipara (Perseverance), Αστεροπη/Asterope (Starry-Faced) and Χρυσοθεμις/Chrysothemis (Golden Custom).[3]

The Pleiades are tangentially connected with the Hesperides in myth as well due to their being the children of Atlas who held Earth and Heaven apart close enough to their garden for Heracles to temporarily take the place of Atlas in his labor to get the Apples of the Hesperides. This is also supported by the fact that during the winter months from November until April, that the Pleiades are readily visible in the evening sky with November being known by some as the "Month of the Pleiades" because of their presence in the sky throughout the night.

The Goddesses of the evening light would be important to the Hellenes because they signal the ending of the day's work and the time when the oikos would gather for their evening meal and storytelling. This is important in the sense of this being the time that communities are bound together and marriages were celebrated during the period.

The Goddesses of the Evening, although not honored after the advent of Christianity in Greece, were still remembered when people would recount the old myths, as well as in both painting and sculpture during the Italian Renaissance. It is safe to say, that their light has never truly been forgotten.

Notes

1 This hymn is still in use during the daily Vespers (Evening) services by the Orthodox Christian Church throughout the world and good translations of this hymn can even be found on Wikipedia as well as at www.goarch.org/chapel/texts in both Greek and English.

2 Hesiod, *Doubtful Frag* 3 (from *Servius On Vergil's Aeneid* 4. 484)

3 www.theoi.com/Titan/Hesperides has a list of these alternate names as well as sources listed for additional names concerning these deities.

<u>Six A.M.</u>

by James B. Nicola

Gray sky bare
save for the
round moon there

I face west
Things look se-
rene, and blessed.

*Memnon, Son of Eos and Tithonus
by Bernard Picart*

Appendix A: Public Domain Hymns to Aurora, Eos, and the Hesperides

Aurora and Eos

Hesiod, Theogony 378 ff (trans. Evelyn-White) (Greek epic C8th or C7th B.C.) :
"And Eos (Dawn) bare to Astraios (Astraeus, the Starry) the strong-hearted Anemoi (Winds), brightening Zephyros (Zephyrus, West Wind), and Boreas (North Wind), headlong in his course, and Notos (Notus, South Wind), — a goddess mating in love with a god. And after these Erigenia (the Early-Born) [Eos] bare the star Eosphoros (Dawn-bringer) [the planet Venus], and the gleaming Astra (Stars) with which heaven is crowned."

Orphic Hymn 78 to Eos (trans. Taylor) (Greek hymns C3rd B.C. to 2nd A.D.) :
"To Eos, Fumigation from Manna. Hear me, O Goddess, whose emerging ray leads on the broad refulgence of the day; blushing Eos (Dawn), whose celestial light beams on the world with reddening splendours bright. Messenger of Titan [Helios the Sun], whom with constant round thy orient beams recall from night profound: labour of every kind to lead it thine, of mortal life the minister divine. Mankind in thee eternally delight, and none presumes to shun thy beauteous sight. Soon as they

splendours break the bands of rest, and eyes unclose, with pleasing sleep oppressed; men, reptiles, birds, and beasts, with general voice, and all the nations of the deep rejoice; for all the culture of our life is thine. Come, blessed power, and to these rites incline: thy holy light increase, and unconfined diffuse its radiance on the mystics' mind."

Ovid, Metamorphoses 7. 700 ff (trans. Melville) (Roman epic C1st B.C. to C1st A.D.) :
"Within two months after our [Kephalos (Cephalus) and Prokris' (Procris')] marriage, while I [Kephalos] spread my nets to catch the antlered deer, the saffron Aurora [Eos the Dawn], above Hymettus' ever-flowery peak, saw me at daybreak as the twilight fled, and carried me away against my will. And may the goddess pardon me, if I say what is true : her rosy cheeks are fair, she rules the borderlands of dark and day, she drinks the nectar's honeydew, but I loved Procris, Procris ever in my heart, and Procris on my lips. I spoke of bonds of holy wedlock, of love's fresh delights, my vows so new and my deserted bride, until in rage the goddess cried : 'Enough of your complaining! Have your Procris! But, if I can see the future, you will rue the day you had her,' and so sent me back. On my way home the goddess' prophecy began to form, fear that my wife had failed her marriage vows . . . Intent on heartbreak I resolved to test her loyalty

with presents. And Aurora [Eos] favoured my fears and changed my form and face (If felt the change) and so I entered Athens unrecognisable and made my way back home . . . [and attempted to seduce his wife in the form of another man. Prokris failed the test and fled him, but the two were eventually reconciled.]

I would go hunting when the sun's first beams coloured the hilltops, as a young man will, roving the woods alone . . . and when my hand had had its fill of sport I used to seek the coolness of the shade and of the breeze, the *aura* breathing from the chilly dales. I sought the gentle *aura* in the heat, I waited for the *aura*, for its balm, my labour's rest. 'Come, *aura*,' I would call, how I remember! 'soothe me, welcome guest, come to my breast, relieve, as is your way, the heat with which I burn.' And I might add, so my fate led me on, more blandishments. 'You comfort and refresh me. For your sake I love the lonely places and the woods; your breath I seek for ever on my lips.'

Some fool who overheard my words mistook the double sense and thought that *aura* (breeze) called so often was the goddess [Aurora, Eos the Dawn], and I in love. This hasty tell-tale hurried off to Procris and told in whispers my supposed offence. Love will believe too soon. In sudden grief she swooned, they told me, then, restored at last, bemoaned her misery, her cruel fate, accused my honour and, imagining a false offence, feared a mere nothing, feared an insubstantial name, poor soul, and grieved as over a true rival paramour. Yet she had doubts and in her wretchedness hoped she was wrong, refusing to accept the tale or, till her eyes had evidence convict her husband of such villainy.

Next day the gleam of dawn had banished night and out into the woods I went and found good sport and, lying on the grass, I called 'Come, *aura* (breeze), come and soothe my weariness! And suddenly, as I spoke, I seemed to hear a sound of moaning, but I called again 'Come, best and loveliest!' A falling leaf made a slight rustle and I thought it was some lurking beast and hurled my [magic never-failing] javelin. It was my wife! Clutching her wounded breast, 'Ay me! Ay me!' she cried. I knew her voice, my Procris' voice, and like a madman rushed headlong towards the sound. And there, half-dead, her clothes blood-splattered, plucking from the wound the gift (heaven help me!) she had given me, I found her . . .

Exhausted then and dying, these few words she forced herself to murmur: 'By our vows of wedlock, by the gods of home and heaven, by my deserts, if I have well deserved, by my death's cause, my own still-living love, I beg you, I implore you, not to take Aura [that is, Aurora or Eos] to be your wife in place of my.' And then at last I learnt of her mistake and told her all. But what did telling help? She slipped away; what little strength was left ebbed with her failing blood; and while her eyes had power still to gaze, she gazed at me, and on my lips her life's last breath was spent; but she looked glad and seemed to die content."

Homeric Hymn 5 to Aphrodite 218 ff (trans. Evelyn-White) (Greek epic C7th - 4th B.C.) :
"So also golden-throned (*khrysothronos*) Eos rapt away Tithonos (Tithonus) who was of your race and like the deathless gods. And she went to ask the dark-clouded Son of Kronos (Cronus) [Zeus] that he should be deathless and live eternally; and Zeus bowed his head to her prayer and fulfilled her desire. Too simple was Lady (*potnia*) Eos: she thought not in her heart to ask for youth for him and to strip him of the slough of deadly age. So while he enjoyed the sweet flower of life he lived rapturously with golden-throned Eos, Erigeneia (Early-Born), by the streams of Okeanos (Oceanus), at the ends of the earth; but when the first grey hairs began to ripple from his comely head and noble chin, Lady Eos kept away from his bed, though she cherished him in her house and nourished him with food and ambrosia and gave him rich clothing. But when loathsome old age pressed full upon him, and he could not move nor lift his limbs, this seemed to her in her heart the best counsel: she laid him in a room and put to the shining doors. There he babbles endlessly, and no more has strength at all, such as once he had in his supple limbs."

Ovid, Metamorphoses 5. 376 ff (trans. Melville) (Roman epic C1st B.C. to C1st A.D.) :

"Aurora [Eos], who had favoured Troy's arms too … a closer trouble, a family grief, had wrung her heart, the loss of Memnon. Slaughtered by Achilles' spear, she, his bright golden mother, saw him dead upon the plain of Troy. The rosy blush that dyes the hour of dawn grew pale and clouds hid the bright heavens. But when his limbs were laid on the last flames, she could not bear to look. With hair unbound, just as she was, she knelt (nor did her pride disdain) before the knees of mighty Jove [Zeus] and pleaded through her tears: 'Least I may be of all the goddesses the golden heavens hold (in all the world my shrines are rarest), yet a deity I am, and I have come not for a gift of fanes or altar-fires or holy days; though should you see how great the services I, but a woman, give when I preserve at each new dawn the boundaries of night, you'd judge some guerdon due. But it's not now Aurora's [Eos'] errand nor her care to claim honours well-earned. I come because my son, Memnon, is lost, who for his uncle's [King Priamos (Priam) of Troy's] sake in vain bore valiant arms and in his first youth (so you willed it) fell to brave Achilles. Grant him, I pray, Ruler of Heaven most high, some honour, solace that he had to die, and soothe a wounded mother's misery!'

Juppiter [Zeus] nodded his assent as Memnon's pyre fell to the leaping flames. Black rolling smoke darkened the daylight, as a stream breathes forth the mist it breeds that lets no sunlight through. Up flew black ashes, and they clustered thick into a single mass, which took a shape and from the fire drew heat and breath of life. Its lightness gave it wings and like a bird at first, and presently a real bird, its great wings whirred and with it sister-birds whirred beyond counting, all from the same source. Three times they circled round the pyre; three times their cries, united, echoed through the air. One the fourth flight the flock split up; then two fierce legions, so divided, fought each other with claws and beaks in full fury, till their wings and battling breasts were weary; then they fell, death-offerings, on the ash whose kin they were, recalling that brave soul from whom they sprang. He who begot them gave those sudden birds their name 'Memnonides' ; and when the sun has coursed through the twelve signs, they fight again to die in memory of Memnon slain … Aurora intent on her own grief: now still her loving sorrow she renews and with her tears the whole wide world bedews."

The Hesperides

Hesiod, Theogony 211 ff (trans. Evelyn-White) (Greek epic C8th or C7th B.C.) :
"And Nyx (Night) bare hateful Moros (Doom) and black Ker (Violent Death) and Thanatos (Death),

and she bare Hypnos (Sleep) and the tribe of Oneiroi (Dreams). And again the goddess murky Nyx, though she lay with none, bare Momos (Blame) and painful Oizys (Misery), and the Hesperides who guard the rich, golden apples and the trees bearing fruit beyond glorious Okeanos (Oceanus). Also she bare the Moirai (Fates) and the ruthless avenging Keres (Death-Fates) … Also deadly Nyx bare Nemesis (Envy) to afflict mortal men, and after her, Apate (Deceit) and Philotes (Friendship) and hateful Geras (Old Age) and hard-hearted Eris (Strife)."

Pseudo-Hyginus, Astronomica 2. 3 (trans. Grant) (Roman mythographer C2nd A.D.) :
"Constellation Serpent … He is said to have guarded the golden apples of the Hesperides, and after Hercules [Herakles] killed him, to have been put by Juno [Hera] among the stars. He is considered the usual watchman of the Gardens of Juno [Hera]. Pherecydes says that when Jupiter [Zeus] wed Juno, Terra (Earth) [Gaia] came, bearing branches with golden apples, and Juno [Hera], in admiration, asked Terra (Earth) to plant them in her gardens near distant Mount Atlas. When Atlas' daughters [the Hesperides] kept picking the apples from the trees, Juno [Hera] is said to have placed this guardian there."

Pseudo-Apollodorus, Bibliotheca 2. 38 - 39 (trans. Aldrich) (Greek mythographer C2nd A.D.):
"Perseus said he would return them [the eye and tooth of Graiai (Graeae)] after they had directed him to the Nymphai (Nymphs) [probably the Hesperides]. These Nymphai had in their possession winged sandals and the *kibisis*, which they say was a knapsack ... They also had the helmet of Haides. When the daughters of Phorkys (Phorcys) had led Perseus to the Nymphai, he returned them their tooth and eye. Approaching the Nymphai he received what he had come for, and he flung on the *kibisis*, tied the sandals on his ankles, and placed the helmet on his head. With the helmet on he could see whomever he cared to look at, but was invisible to others."

Apollonius Rhodius, Argonautica 4. 1390 ff (trans. Rieu) (Greek epic C3rd B.C.) :
"[The Argonauts port their ship across the Libyan desert :] They set her [the ship Argo] down from their sturdy shoulders in the Tritonian lagoon. Once there, it was their first concern to slake the burning thirst that was added to their aches and pains. They dashed off, like mad dogs, in search of fresh water; and they were fortunate. They [the Argonauts] found the sacred plot where, till the day before, the serpent Ladon, a son of the Libyan soil, had kept watch over the golden apples in the Garden of Atlas, while close at hand and busy at their tasks the

Hesperides sang their lovely song. But now the snake, struck down by Herakles, lay by the trunk of the apple-tree. Only the tip of his tail was still twitching; from the head down, his dark spine showed not a sign of life. His blood had been poisoned by arrows steeped in the gall of the Hydra Lernaia (Lernaean), and flies perished in the festering wounds.

Close by, with their white arms flung over their golden heads, the Hesperides were wailing as the Argonauts approached. The whole company came on them suddenly, and in a trice the Nymphai (Nymphs) turned to dust and earth on the spot where they had stood. Orpheus, seeing the hand of Heaven in this, addressed a prayer to them on behalf of his comrades: 'Beautiful and beatific Powers, Queens indeed, be kind to us, whether Olympos or the underworld counts you among its goddesses, or whether you prefer the name of Solitary Nymphai. Come, blessed Spirits, Daughters of Okeanos (Oceanus), make yourselves manifest to our expectant eyes and lead us to a place where we can quench this burning, never-ending thirst with fresh water springing from a rock or gushing from the ground. And if ever we bring home our ship into an Akhaian (Achaean) port, we will treat you as we treat the greatest goddesses, showing our gratitude with innumberable gifts of wine and offerings at the festal board.'

Orpheus sobbed as he prayed. But the Nymphai were still at hand, and they took pity on the suffering men. They wrought a miracle. First, grass sprung up from the ground, then long shoots appeared above the grass, and in a moment three saplings, tall, straight and in full leaf, were growing there. Hespere (Hespera) became a poplar; Erytheis an elm; Aigle (Aegle) a sacred willow. Yet they were still themselves; the trees could not conceal their former shapes--that was the greatest wonder of all. And now the Argonauts heard Aigle in her gentle voice tell them what they wished to know.

'You have indeed been fortunate,' she said. 'There was a man here yesterday, an evil man, who killed the watching Snake, stole our golden apples, and is gone. To us he brought unspeakable sorrow; to you release from suffering. He was a savage brute, hideous to look at; a cruel man, with glaring eyes and scowling face. He wore the skin of an enormous lion and carried a great club of olive-wood and the bow and arrows with which he shot our monster here. It appeared that he, like you, had come on foot and was parched with thirst. For he rushed about the place in search of water; but with no success, till he found the rock that you see over there near to the Tritonian lagoon. Then it occurred to him, or he was prompted by a god, to tap the base of the rock. He struck it with his foot, water gushed out, and he fell on his hands and chest and drank greedily from the cleft till, with his head down like a beast in the fields, he had filled his mighty paunch.'

The Minyai were delighted. They ran off in happy haste towards the place where Aigle had pointed out the spring."

Colluthus, Rape of Helen 58 ff (trans. Mair) (Greek poetry C5th to C6th A.D.) :
"[Eris was enraged at being turned away from the wedding of Peleus and Thetis :] And now she bethought her of the golden apples of the Hesperides. Thence Eris took the fruit that should be the harbinger of war, even the apple, and devised the scheme of signal woes. Whirling her arm she hurled into the banquet the primal seed of turmoil and disturbed the choir of goddesses. Hera, glorying to be the spouse and to share the bed of Zeus, rose up amazed, and would fain have seized it. And Kypris (Cypris) [Aphrodite], as being more excellent than all, desired to have the apple, for that it is the treasure of the Erotes (Loves). But Hera would not give it up and Athena would not yield."

Appendix B: Recommended Reading

Apollonius Rhodius. *Argonautica* 1, 3, 4
Bacchylides. *Fragment* 13
Cicero. *On the Nature of the Gods* 3.17
Colluthus. *The Rape of Helen* 58 ff
Euripides. *Hippolytus* 742 ff
Greek Lyric V Fragment 1023
Hesiod. *Theogony* 371, 378
Homer. *The Homeric Hymns: To Aphrodite V* and *To Helios XXXI* and *The Iliad* 23.226 and *The Odyssey* 5
Nonnus. *Dionysiaca* 5, 6, 11, 18, 44, 47, 138, 299
Orpheus. *The Orphic Hymns: To Eos LXXVII*
Ovid. *Fasti* 4, 5 and *Metamorphoses* 7
Pseudo-Apollodorus. *Bibliotheca* 1, 3
Pseudo-Hyginus. *Astronomica* 2.3 and *Fabulae* 189, 270
Quintas Smyrnaeus. *Posthomerica: The Fall of Troy Book II*
Sappho. *Fragment* 58, 104
Statius. *Thebaid* 2.134 ff
Virgil. *Georgics* 1.246 ff

Appendix C: Our Contributors

Rebecca Buchanan is the editor-in-chief of *Bibliotheca Alexandrina*, and the editor of *Eternal Haunted Summer*. She has released two short story collections through *Asphodel Press*: *A Witch Among Wolves, And Other Pagan Tales*; and *The Serpent in the Throat, And Other Pagan Tales*.

Amanda Artemisia Forrester is currently working on building the Missouri homestead of her dreams. She is the author of *Ink In My Veins: A Collection of Contemporary Pagan Poetry*, and *Songs of Praise: Hymns to the Gods of Greece*. She is working on the forthcoming *Journey to Olympos: A Modern Spiritual Odyssey* (which has been a 10-year, off and on project). A self-labeled history geek, she has taught classes on Greek Mythology, contacting your spirit guides, and has written and taught the coursework for "Olympos in Egypt", an introduction to the unique hybrid culture and spiritually that grew up in Alexandria, Egypt in the Hellenistic Age. In a few years when the homestead is up and running, she may make it her goal to begin teaching again and holding rituals on her five acre property, Artemis Acres, and to reestablish the Temple of Athena the Savior (formerly of South Bend, Indiana) in Missouri. She enjoys writing, reading, worshiping the Gods, teaching, drawing, painting, gardening, walking in the woods, engaging in various fantasy and sci-fi fandoms, and caring for the far too many animals who find their way to her home. She has previously been published in many *Bibliotheca Alexandrina* anthologies; the Salt Lake City Pagan Literacy collection, *Enhedunna;* and the ezine *Eternal Haunted Summer*. Her blog can be found at templeofathena.wordpress.com, and she runs a Cafepress store, OtherWorld Creations, at cafepress.com/other_world.

Laurie Goodhart has been pursuing the mythic and ethereal as an artist, and the fundamental earth processes as an organic farmer, for 40 years. Her artwork has been published in print books and periodicals for decades, and hundreds of pieces are in private collections. A full resume and dozens of images of available paintings and prints are at lauriegoodhart.net.

Anne Hatzakis is a mother, a college student, and a blogger about the Hellenic Theoi [blog address www.greekrevivalistmommy.com]. She is working on a book about the Delphic Maxims in her limited free time as well as a series of monthly devotional booklets for the Hellenic Theoi. Both of these projects have an indefinite release timetable because of the demands of being a mother and college student.

Chris Hubbard first started on his spiritual path in his teens, studying alchemy, gnosticism, and the Kabbalah. Anymore, he enjoys writing, watching movies, and trying to live the ways of the Tao in daily life.

Iris is a member of Blue Star and Hellenion and has been a practicing pagan for thirty years. She lives in a non-traditional family with five other adults, one tweenager, five cats and a hedgehog.

Moscow-born **Nina Kossman** is an artist, writer, poet, playwright. Her paintings and sculptures have been exhibited in Moscow and New York. The recipient of a National Endowment for the Arts fellowship, a UNESCO/PEN Short Story Award, grants from Foundation for Hellenic Culture and Alexander S. Onassis Public Benefit Foundation, she is the author of two books of poems in Russian and English, as well as the translator of two volumes of Marina Tsvetaeva's poetry. Her other publications include *Behind the Border* (*HarperCollins*, 1994) and *Gods and Mortals: Modern Poems on Classical Myths* (*Oxford University Press*, 2001). Her work has been translated into several languages, including Japanese, Dutch, Greek, and Spanish. She lives in New York.

Jennifer Lawrence has followed the gods of Greece, Ireland, and the Northlands for decades now; she is a member of Hellenion, The Troth, Ár nDraíocht Féin, and Ord Brigideach. After earning a B.A. in Literature and a B.S. in Criminal Justice, she went on to work as an editor for Jupiter Gardens Press, a small publishing company in the Midwest. Her interests include history, gardening, herbalism, mythology and fairy tales, hiking, camping, and the martial arts. Her work has appeared in numerous publications, including *Aphelion*, *Jabberwocky*, *Cabinet Des Fees*, *Goblin Fruit*, *Idunna*, *Oak Leaves,* and many devotional anthologies.

Gerri Leen lives in Northern Virginia and originally hails from Seattle. In addition to being an avid reader and an at-times sporadic writer, she's passionate about horse racing (the racing part, not betting), tea, whiskey, handbags, and art. She has work appearing in: *Nature, Orson Scott Card's Intergalactic Medicine Show*, *Daily Science Fiction*, *Grievous Angel*, *Grimdark,* and others, and has edited several anthologies for independent presses. See more at http://www.gerrileen.com.

Claire Manning is a solitary eclectic witch based in London, England. She has been practicing for nearly two decades and is currently in her final year of training with the Temple of Witchcraft where she also serves as a teaching assistant and mentor. A perpetual student, Claire can often be found curled up with a large cup of tea and her nose planted firmly in a book.

James B. Nicola's poems have appeared nine time in previous anthologies from *Bibliotheca Alexandrina*, as well as in the *Antioch*, *Southwest* and *Atlanta Reviews*, *Rattle*, *Tar River*, and *Poetry East,* and in many journals in Europe and Canada. A Yale graduate, he won a Dana Literary Award, a *Willow Review* award, and a People's Choice award (from *Storyteller*), and he was featured poet at *New Formalist*. His nonfiction book, *Playing the Audience,* won a *Choice* award. His first full-length poetry collection is *Manhattan Plaza* (2014); his second, *Stage to Page: Poems from the Theater* (June 2016). His poetry collections are *Manhattan Plaza* (2014), *Stage to Page* (2016), *Wind in the Cave* (2017), and the upcoming *Out of Nothing: Poems of Art and Artists* (2018).

John "Apollonius" Opsopaus, PhD has practiced magic, divination, and Neopaganism since the 1960s. He has some fifty publications in various magical and Neopagan magazines. He designed the Pythagorean Tarot and wrote the comprehensive *Guide to the Pythagorean Tarot* (*Llewellyn*, 2001), and his *Oracles of Apollo* (*Llewellyn*, 2017) teaches divination based on ancient texts that he has translated. Opsopaus frequently presents workshops on Hellenic magic and Neopaganism, Pythagorean theurgy, divination, and related topics. In the early 1990s he founded the Omphalos, a networking organization for Neopagans in the Greek and Roman traditions and one of the first Internet resources for them. He is past coordinator of the Scholars Guild for the Church of All Worlds, past Arkhon of the Hellenic Kin of ADF (A Druid Fellowship), and a member of the Grey Council. His writings can be found at omphalos.org/BA

Ariadni Rainbird writes: The Greek Gods have always been with me, from my earliest memories when the Greek myths were my favourite childhood bedtime stories. My contact with the Hellenic Gods, Hellenic influence on British culture and Hellenic thought continued through my school days from the study of the English poets, where the Gods of Greece and Rome make frequent appearances, to my University days with the study of Ancient Greek drama and philosophy. I have been involved in the pagan/polytheist scene for over 30 years, initially Training as a Priestess in the Fellowship of Isis, then initiation into a Wiccan coven, running covens for many years and also dipping in to Buddhism, Hinduism, Druidry and Asatru, before finally deciding that I wanted to dedicate myself to the Hellenic path. Over the past few years I have followed an Orphic path, and am in the process of helping to set up the Hellenic Pagan Association

UK to be the first national Hellenic Pagan organisation in the UK.

Zachariah Shipman has been a devoted Hellenic Polytheist since the young age of ten years old. Now, as an eighteen year-old devotee of Dionysos, he is involved directly with the non-profitable organization known as United Hellenismos Association, where he was elected the Director of Education.

Gregory Stires is a short story author and poet. He has been writing poetry since the 9th grade and has no previous publications. While he is more experienced in writing poetry and short stories, he also is very knowledgeable in many mythologies of the world such as those of Egyptian, Greco-Roman, and Norse mythology.

Gareth Writer-Davies writes: Shortlisted for the Bridport Prize (2014 and 2017) and the Erbacce Prize (2014). Commended in the Prole Laureate Competition (2015) and Prole Laureate for 2017. Commended in the Welsh Poetry Competition (2015) and Highly Commended in 2017. His pamphlet *Bodies*, was published in 2015 by *Indigo Dreams* and the pamphlet *Cry Baby* came out in November 2017.

Appendix D:
About Bibliotheca Alexandrina

Ptolemy Soter, the first Makedonian ruler of Egypt, established the library at Alexandria to collect all of the world's learning in a single place. His scholars compiled definitive editions of the Classics, translated important foreign texts into Greek, and made monumental strides in science, mathematics, philosophy and literature. By some accounts over a million scrolls were housed in the famed library, and though it has long since perished due to the ravages of war, fire, and human ignorance, the image of this great institution has remained as a powerful inspiration down through the centuries.

To help promote the revival of traditional polytheistic religions we have launched a series of books dedicated to the ancient gods of Greece and Egypt. The library is a collaborative effort drawing on the combined resources of the different elements within the modern Hellenic and Kemetic communities, in the hope that we can come together to praise our gods and share our diverse understandings, experiences and approaches to the divine.

A list of our current and forthcoming titles can be found on the following page. For more information on the Bibliotheca, our submission requirements for upcoming devotionals, or to learn about our organization, please visit us at neosalexandria.org.

Sincerely,

The Editorial Board
of the Library of Neos Alexandria

Current Titles
    Written in Wine: A Devotional Anthology for Dionysos
    Dancing God: Poetry of Myths and Magicks
    Goat Foot God
    Longing for Wisdom: The Message of the Maxims
    The Phillupic Hymns
    Unbound: A Devotional Anthology for Artemis
    Waters of Life: A Devotional Anthology for Isis and Serapis
    Bearing Torches: A Devotional Anthology for Hekate
    Queen of the Great Below: An Anthology in Honor of Ereshkigal
    From Cave to Sky: A Devotional Anthology in Honor of Zeus
    Out of Arcadia: A Devotional Anthology for Pan

Anointed: A Devotional Anthology for the Deities of the Near and Middle East

The Scribing Ibis: An Anthology of Pagan Fiction in Honor of Thoth

Queen of the Sacred Way: A Devotional Anthology in Honor of Persephone

Unto Herself: A Devotional Anthology for Independent Goddesses

The Shining Cities: An Anthology of Pagan Science Fiction

Guardian of the Road: A Devotional Anthology in Honor of Hermes

Harnessing Fire: A Devotional Anthology in Honor of Hephaestus

Beyond the Pillars: An Anthology of Pagan Fantasy

Queen of Olympos: A Devotional Anthology for Hera and Iuno

A Mantle of Stars: A Devotional Anthology in Honor of the Queen of Heaven

Crossing the River: An Anthology in Honor of Sacred Journeys

Ferryman of Souls: A Devotional for Charon

By Blood, Bone, and Blade: A Tribute to the Morrigan

Potnia: An Anthology in Honor of Demeter

The Queen of the Sky Who Rules Over All the Gods: A Devotional Anthology in Honor of Bast

From the Roaring Deep: A Devotional for Poseidon and the Spirits of the Sea

Daughter of the Sun: A Devotional Anthology in Honor of Sekhmet

Seasons of Grace: A Devotional in Honor of the Muses, the Charites, and the Horae

Lunessence: A Devotional for Selene

Les Cabinets des Polythéistes: An Anthology of Pagan Fairy Tales, Folktales, and Nursery Rhymes

With Lyre and Bow: A Devotional in Honor of Apollo

Garland of the Goddess: Tales and Poems of the Feminine Divine

The Dark Ones: Tales and Poems of the Shadow Gods

First and Last: A Devotional for Hestia

Dauntless: A Devotional in Honor of Ares and Mars

Blood and Roses: A Devotional for Aphrodite and Venus

At the Gates of Dawn and Dusk: A Devotional for Aurora, Eos, and the Hesperides

Forthcoming Titles

The Far-Shining One: A Devotional for Helios and the Spirits of the Sun

A Silver Sun and Inky Clouds: A Devotional for Djehuty and Set

Lord of the Carnelian Temple: A Devotional in Honor of Sobek

Lord of the Horizon: A Devotional in Honor of Horus

Lady of the Sycamore: A Devotional in Honor of Hathor

The Diviner's Handbook: Writings on Ancient and Modern Divination Practices

With an Adamantine Sickle: A Devotional for the Titans

Among Satyrs and Nymphs: A Devotional Anthology to Hellenic Nature Spirits

Made in United States
Troutdale, OR
08/03/2023